Germany

For Kids

People, Places and Cultures

Children Explore The World Books

BABY PROFESSOR
EDUCATION KIDS

Speedy Publishing LLC
40 E. Main St. #1156
Newark, DE 19711
www.speedypublishing.com

Let's learn some interesting facts about Germany!

The name for Germany in the German language is Deutschland.

The capital of Germany is Berlin, it is also the largest city.

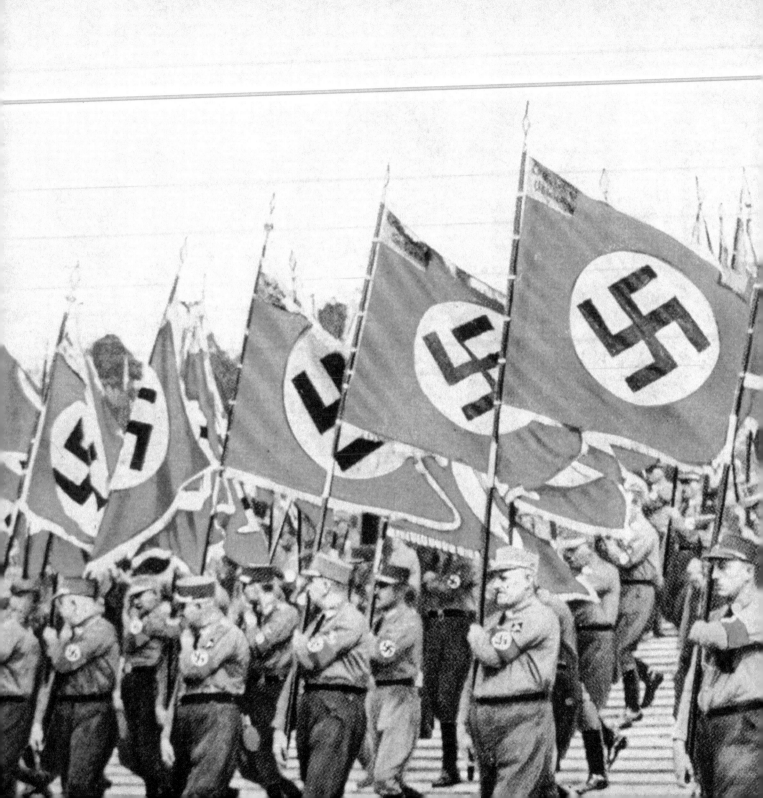

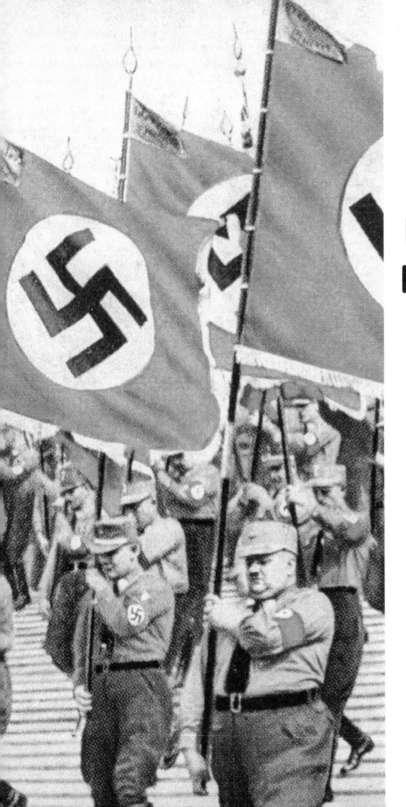

Germany has had an unsettled history, including the Nazi regime and tension between East and West Germany (which were reunified in 1990).

Germany has the largest economy in Europe.

Germany has a number of important natural resources, including copper, nickel, natural gas, uranium and coal.

Over 100 Germans have been awarded the Nobel prize in their field, including Albert Einstein, who was born in Germany.

Football (soccer) is the most popular sport in Germany.

The highest mountain in Germany is the 'Zugspitze' (which means 'windy peak') with 2,963 metres (roughly 10,000 feet).

Germans love going to the museums, concerts and theatres.

Germany shares borders with nine other countries – Denmark, Poland, the Czech Republic, Austria, Switzerland, France, Belgium, Luxembourg and the Netherlands.

About two-thirds of the population are Christian – split evenly between Protestant and Catholic, but you'll find more Protestants in the north and more Catholics in the south. There are around 4 million Muslims and 100,000 Jews.

Germany is one of the world's leading book nations – publishing around 94,000 titles every year.

Smoking is banned in public places but drinking is still legal – smoking has been banned in public buildings, on public transportation and in other places since 2007 but you can drink alcohol openly.

The Germans love their bread, which is mainly a mix of wheat and rye flour and is much darker and has a hard crust. Bread rolls are also eaten.

Germany's forests, the Black Forest and the Bavarian Forest, are home to wild pig, fox, and deer.

The castle is built in the Bavarian Alps of Germany. Neuschwanstein is the most famous of three castles built by Louis II of Bavaria, also known as Mad King Louis.

Oktoberfest is a traditional festival that Germans have every year.

Germany has a lot to offer and you should visit the country soon and explore!

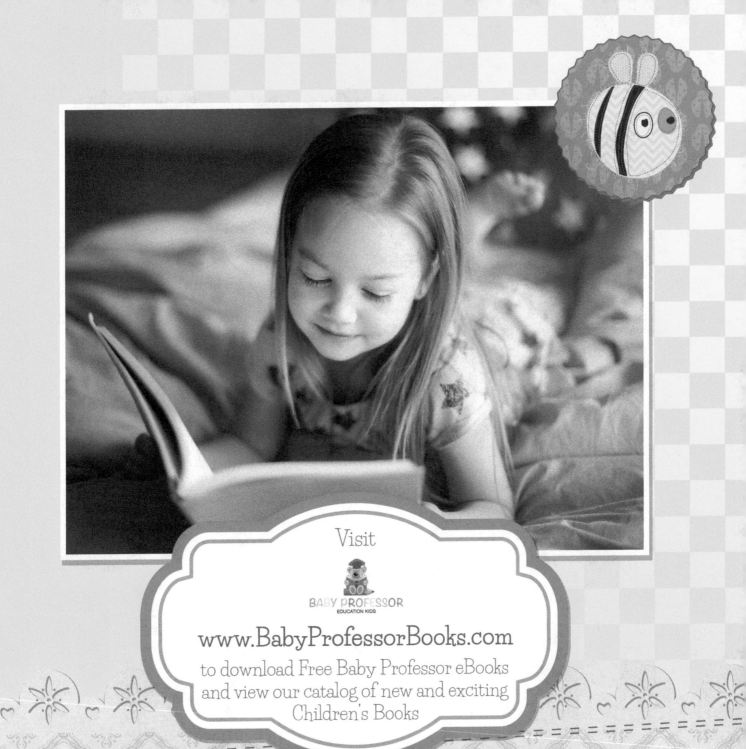

Visit

BABY PROFESSOR
EDUCATION KIDS

www.BabyProfessorBooks.com

to download Free Baby Professor eBooks
and view our catalog of new and exciting
Children's Books

CPSIA information can be obtained
at www.ICGtesting.com
Printed in the USA
BVHW091312191222
654540BV00010B/637

9 781683 056126